Denzel
Washington

Mike Wilson

Published in association with The Basic Skills Agency

Hodder & Stoughton

A MEMBER OF THE HODDER HEADLINE GROUP

Acknowledgements

Cover: Al Seib/The LA Times © LA Times/Retna Ltd.

Photos: p. 2 © PA PHOTOS/EPA; pp. 8, 19 © The Ronald Grant Archive; p. 12 © BFI Stills; p. 16 © Russell Mulcahy/bfi Collections; p. 24 © Trapper Frank/CORBIS SYGMA; p. 27 © The Kobal Collection

Orders: please contact Bookpoint Ltd, 130 Milton Park, Abingdon, Oxon OX14 4SB. Telephone: (44) 01235 827720. Fax: (44) 01235 400454. Lines are open from 9.00–6.00, Monday to Saturday, with a 24 hour message answering service. You can also order through our website www.hodderheadline.co.uk.

British Library Cataloguing in Publication Data
A catalogue record for this title is available from the British Library

ISBN 0 340 87654 9

First Published 2003
Impression number   10 9 8 7 6 5 4 3 2 1
Year   2007 2006 2005 2004 2003

Typeset by Fakenham Phososetting Limited Fakenham Norfolk
Printed in Great Britain for Hodder & Stoughton Educational, a division of Hodder Headline, 338 Euston Road, London NW1 3BH by The Bath Press Ltd, Bath.

Contents

1 Denzel

It was 24 March, 2002.

Three black actors stood proudly
on a stage in Hollywood.

The three had joined
the Hollywood Greats.
They each held an Oscar
in their hands.

One was Halle Berry.
She was the first black actress
ever to win a Best Actress Oscar.

By her side was Sidney Poitier.
He won an Oscar
for his 40 years in Hollywood.

The other man was Denzel Washington.

Denzel and Halle Berry with their Oscars.

Denzel stood there smiling.

He looked tall, handsome
and very proud.

He said:
'God is good, God is great.
If you wish for something good,
deep in your heart,
God will make that dream come true.
But in my wildest dreams,
I never wished for a night like this.
It's been amazing.
An amazing journey
with an amazing end.'

That was just like Denzel.
He never dreamed of getting an Oscar.

But he had been up for an Oscar before –
in 1987 for *Cry Freedom*,
in 1993 for *Malcolm X*,
and 1999 for *The Hurricane*.

In 1989, he won an Oscar
for Best Supporting Actor.
That was for *Glory*.

So Denzel is pretty modest.
He knows that success
does not come easy.
You have to work hard for it.

He's really just a normal guy
doing the best he can at his job.
It's just that his job is being cool,
calm and confident under pressure.

And being very good-looking in movies.

2 Dr. Denzel

Denzel Washington
was born in New York
on 23 December 1954.

Denzel was his dad's name too.
His dad got the name from Dr. Denzel,
who was the doctor at his birth.

Denzel's dad was a preacher
and a man of God.
His mum worked in a beauty salon.

Denzel was the second of three children.
He grew up a happy boy.
He loved the stories his dad told in church.
He loved it when his dad
put on an act to bring the stories alive.

When Denzel was just 14,
he was sent to boarding school.
His mum and dad had split up.
Later, they got divorced.

But Denzel didn't let it get to him.
He still grew up with a strong faith in God,
and a strong faith in the family.

After school,
Denzel went to college in New York.
He wanted to be a journalist,
or maybe a doctor.

But one year, at summer camp,
Denzel had a go at acting
for the first time.

It was easy.
It was fun.

Denzel was good looking,
tall and strong.
He had power and presence.
He had talent.
He was a natural.

In those early college plays,
everyone raved about him.

Denzel won a place
at a top drama school
in San Francisco.

He got his degree.
But by now,
he wanted to be an actor.

After just one year at drama school,
Denzel started looking for acting work.

It didn't take long.
His first big break came in 1982.
He got the part of Dr. Chandler
in *St. Elsewhere*.
St. Elsewhere was a TV drama
set in a hospital.

Dr. Phillip Chandler
was tall, calm and very good-looking.
He was everything a TV doctor should be!

Denzel stayed at *St. Elsewhere*
for six years.

When he left, in 1988,
he was already a movie star.

Denzel as Dr. Chandler in *St. Elsewhere*.

Denzel went on to play
those cool, calm, strong men
over and over again.
In every movie,
he's always powerful and intense.

Sometimes he plays the bad guy.
But he's nearly always the hero.

He's been a Black Hero
in some movies.
He's been an Action Hero,
and he's been in a wheelchair.
He's been a soldier, a lawyer, a cop.
And he's been a Romantic Hero . . .

But the real Denzel Washington
is just a quiet, normal guy.
Off screen, the part he likes to play
is Family Man.

3 Black Hero

In 1987, Denzel was in *Cry Freedom*.

Cry Freedom was an important movie
for black people all over the world.

Denzel played Steve Biko,
a black leader in South Africa
in the 1970s.
Back then,
South Africa was still a racist state.

Steve Biko was beaten and killed
in prison by police in 1977.

In 1992, Denzel played another black leader –
in the film *Malcolm X*.

It was the true story of Malcolm Little,
a small-time no-hoper black American,
born in 1925.

He drifted into crime
and ended up in prison.
In prison, he learned about black history,
black politics and Islam.

He changed his name to Malcolm X.
'Little' was the name his family was given
by white slave-owners.
Malcolm X led the fight
against racism in America.
He led the Black Power movement.
He was too violent for white America,
but not violent enough
for some black Americans.

He was gunned down and killed
by other black Muslims in 1965.

Like Steve Biko, he became a hero
for black people everywhere.

Denzel in *Malcolm X.*

4 A Different Type of Hero

Denzel was back in prison again
when he made *The Hurricane*.
The Hurricane was another true story
about a black hero.
Rubin Carter was a boxer,
and 'Hurricane' was his nickname.

Denzel worked out for a year
before the film.
He wanted to be in good shape
for the fight scenes.

Hurricane Carter was framed,
by a racist cop,
for murders he didn't commit.
He spent nearly twenty years in jail.

In the end,
he got out with a pardon.
So it was a sort of happy ending.

But it was a sad, powerful story.
Hurricane Carter put up with his years in prison
with dignity and pride.

He was a different type of Black Hero.
He was not like Malcolm X,
who wanted black people to fight back.

Hurricane Carter had been a boxer.
But he came to know
that fighting was not the answer.

Denzel has played the black hero
in three important movies.

(And he named one of his sons Malcolm,
after Malcolm X.)

But he doesn't want to be typecast.
There's more to Denzel than that.

'I'm very proud to be black,'
he says.
'But black is not *all* I am.'

There are plenty of other good parts
for a man with his looks
and his talent as an actor.

5 Action Hero

Sometimes, Denzel gets to be in an action movie.
He got to show off his muscles
in movies like *Ricochet* (1991),
The Siege (1998),
and *Courage Under Fire* (1996).

But Denzel's action movies
are not just about guns and girls
and bombs and car-chases.
They have brains
as well as muscles.
There's tension, drama
and powerful acting.

In *Glory* (1989)
Denzel was a runaway slave.
He becomes a soldier
in the US Civil War.

Denzel won an Oscar
for Best Supporting Actor.

Denzel in *Ricochet*.

In *The Siege*,
Denzel heads a US Task Force
fighting a terrorist bomb attack.

For the first time,
a Hollywood movie was about
the fear of terrorist attack
on American soil.

The Siege was made in 1998.
This was three years before
the real terrorist attacks
on New York and Washington
on September 11, 2001.

6 Bad Guy

Denzel doesn't get to play the Bad Guy very often.
But when he does,
he's very good at it!

He made *Training Day*,
a police thriller, in 2002.

Denzel was Alonzo Harris.
He's been an LA cop for the last ten years.
He makes up the rules as he goes along.

'We're the cops,' he explains.
'We can do what the hell we want!'

In one scene, Alonzo kills a drug dealer.
But he just knows
he's doing the right thing:

'He sold kids drugs.
The world is a better place without him.'

Denzel as Alonzo Harris in *Training Day* (with Ethan Hawke).

Alonzo is a problem for the other LA cops.

Is he really keeping crime off the streets?
Or is he just as bad as the bad guys?

This is the sort of question
that makes you think.
This is what makes a movie interesting to Denzel.

Good cop or bad cop,
Denzel did a good job on *Training Day*.
This was the part
that won him his Oscar for Best Actor.

7 Romantic Hero

In a lot of movies,
Denzel gets to play the love interest.

He was a handsome prince
in Shakespeare's
Much Ado About Nothing (1993).

And *Mississippi Masala* (1991)
was a love story
between an African-American man
and an Asian-American woman.

Even in thrillers
like *The Pelican Brief* (1993),
Devil In A Blue Dress (1995)
and *The Preacher's Wife* (1996),
romance is never very far away
between him and his leading lady.

The trouble is,
Denzel is just too good-looking!

As a child,
Denzel had a gap in his front teeth.
Now that's been sorted,
he's perfect!

Fans are always voting him
one of the most sexy men in Hollywood.

How does Denzel feel about that?

Well, he's pretty modest, as usual.

'I'm just a normal man,' he says.
'I'm just trying to <u>be</u> good.
I don't worry about <u>looking</u> good!'

That's easy for him to say:

In 1990, Denzel was in the Top 50
Most Beautiful People
(in the US *People* magazine).

Twelve years later, in 2002,
he was still in the Top 50
Most Beautiful People!

8 Family Man

The part Denzel likes to play the most
is Family Man.

He met his wife, Pauletta, in 1977.
They were both working on a TV movie.

They were married in 1983,
and now have four kids:
David (born 1984),
Katia (born 1987),
and the twins Malcolm and Olivia
(born 1991).

Denzel is serious about his work.
But he's more serious about his family:

'Acting is not life,' he says.
'It's just a job.
Those children are life.
I don't want to be the man who says –
I wasn't there for my kids.
I was too busy thinking of myself.
I didn't think about my kids.'

Denzel with his wife, Pauletta.

Denzel says it can be hard
working in Hollywood.

'Being a star,
it's easy to get tempted.
But my family is everything to me.'

In 1995, Denzel and Pauletta
were on a trip to South Africa.
They renewed their wedding vows,
and promised to remain faithful.

9 Director Hero

In 2002, Denzel was back at work
playing the part of a doctor again.

He played the psychiatrist
Dr Davenport, in the movie *Antwone Fisher*.

It's based on a true story:
Antwone Fisher is sent
to Dr Davenport
to sort out his problems with anger.

Antwone had a hard time in foster care
when he was a child.

Denzel did a good job in front of the camera.
But he was in charge behind the camera too.

Antwone Fisher was the first movie
with Denzel as director.

'It was difficult,' says Denzel.
'It was hard work,
being the director and a leading actor.
But I like hard work!'

Denzel the director.

It must be true.

Denzel Washington
works harder than most Hollywood stars.

He's played a wide range of Hollywood heroes.
But the part he plays best
is the normal, loving husband and dad.

Oh, and the handsome devil.

'I don't aim to please my public,'
he has said.
'I only do movies that interest me.'

Where next
for one of Hollywood's
Most Beautiful People?